Hayden Williams

THE
FASHION
ACTIVITY BOOK

ilex

T0305008

When I was a little boy, I spent hours crafting my own paper dolls. I would design their outfits, carefully cut them out and stick my creations together. I drew inspiration from the fashion dolls I collected (and still do!) and I dreamed of one day designing my own dolls. As I got older, I began to create my own fashion illustrations and post them online. And to my surprise, many people loved them as much as I did. Since then, I've had the chance to work with people across the fashion industry to turn my dream designs into reality.

Now, as a full-time fashion illustrator, I am lucky enough to design outfits for a living. What I love most about my job is the increased creativity that comes from sharing my work, and the satisfaction of creating pieces that people want to wear. In this activity book, I want to share the creative process with you – you can colour in and customize my designs, as well as use the unclothed mannequins dotted throughout the book to experiment with your own designs, and even cut out and dress up the paper dolls at the back of the book.

Many of the illustrations in this book are brand new and exclusive pieces, while others are classics from my archives. They take inspiration from some of my favourite eras and aesthetics, ranging from 40s and 50s old-school Hollywood glamour to pop culture and the more current fashion styles of today. The book is divided into the four seasons, so you'll find pieces for all times of year. Look out for:

DAY ENSEMBLES
These outfits capture on-the-go chic style. Your model could be on her way to a meeting, going shopping or running errands... Whatever she's doing, she'll be looking fabulous!

HAUTE COUTURE
Gorgeous, gorgeous gowns. You'll find a treasure trove of glamorous dresses that are red-carpet-ready for you to customize as you please. Get creative with colour palettes and prints to design something worthy of the Met Gala.

BEAUTY
Lips, eyes, cheeks, face! Creating the perfect makeup look can be just as much fun as designing an outfit. Take the opportunity to focus on the faces of some of the models in this book, and bring them to life with foundation, eyeshadow, blush, lipstick and more.

POP CULTURE
I am continually inspired by moments from movies and TV. In particular, look out for nods to my favourite Hollywood starlets and icons.

HALLOWEEN
Spooky season is my favourite season! Many of my designs are inspired by fantasy and myth. From ghosts to fembots, mermaids to aliens, I thrive creatively during Halloween, and enjoy leaning into the campness of 'haunt' couture.

SO GET YOUR PENS & PENCILS RUNWAY READY & PREPARE TO UNLEASH YOUR INNER FASHION DESIGNER!

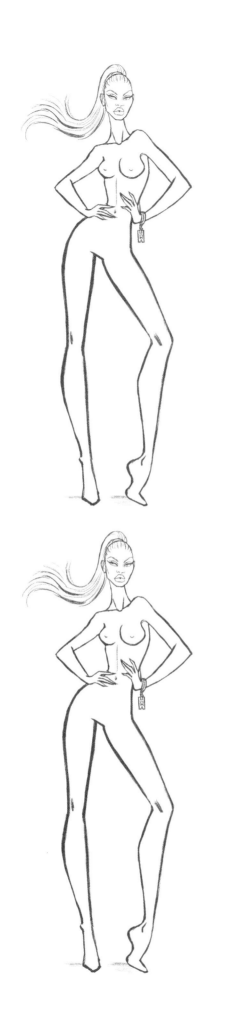
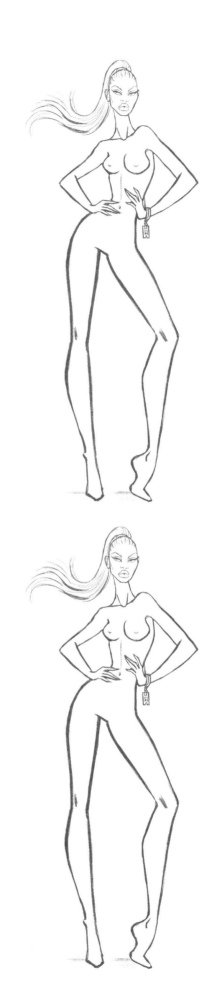

SUMMER

SUMMER

SUMMER

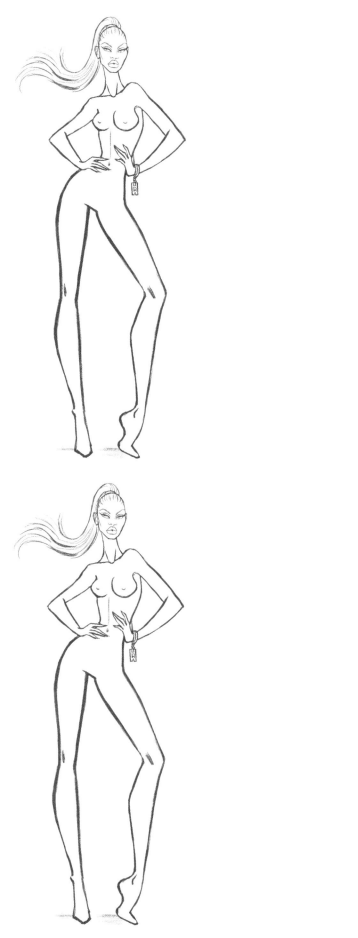

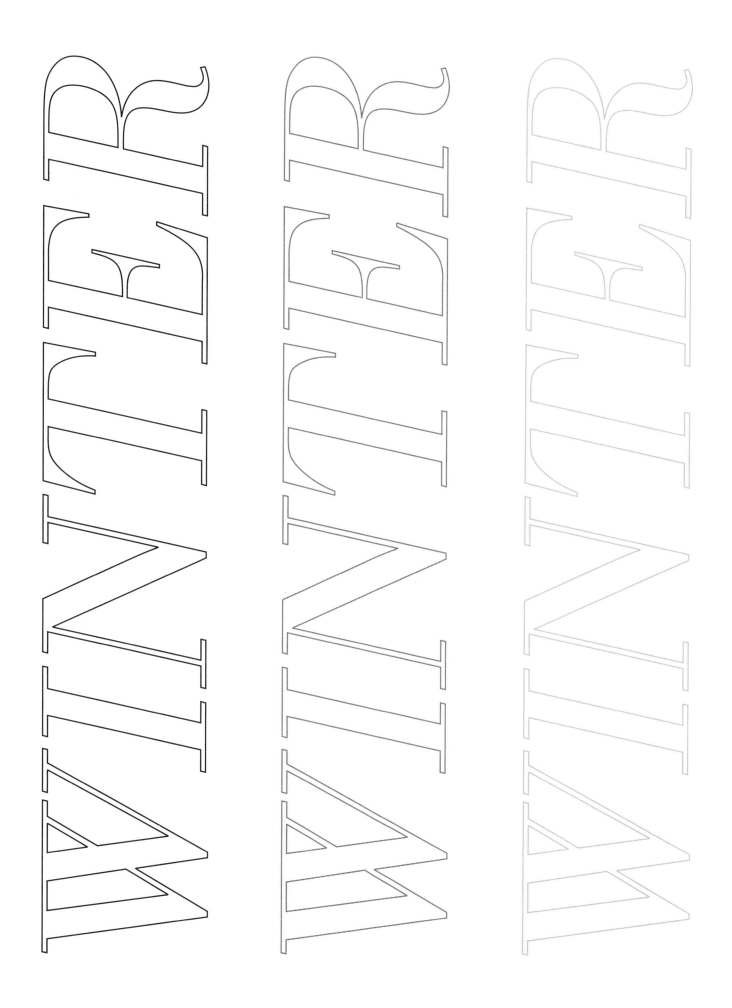

Acknowledgements

It is with profound gratitude and a deep sense of accomplishment that I embrace the title of officially being a published author! This is a very surreal feeling and I am so proud of the hard work and passion that I poured into this project. I truly hope it sparks much creativity and enjoyment for many people.

I would like to say a huge thank you to the entire incredible team at Octopus Publishing Group for giving me this opportunity and for their hard work in helping me put together and publish my first ever book. They believed in my story and vision from the very first meeting we had and it's been truly special collaborating with a team that is as passionate about this project as I am.

Thank you to my family – my mother Tina, father Charles and my sister Serena – for nurturing my artistic talent and pursuits from a very tender age. Your encouragement and unwavering faith in me through all the highs and lows has helped lay the foundation for my achievements, but is also the reason I am humbly grateful for the success I have achieved thus far. My love for you all is beyond words.

Thank you to my closest friends, whose genuine support and encouragement has been a constant source of motivation. Having intrinsically good people in my life is a true blessing and your presence on this journey has been invaluable.

Thank you to Samuel Kasumu for connecting me with the team at Octopus and for being so supportive.

Last but not least, thank you to all of the people who have followed and supported my career as a fashion illustrator/designer for over a decade. I am so blessed to be able to share my work with so many who love and appreciate the dedication and passion I put into my creative endeavours. Your enduring support means the world to me.

This book represents more than a milestone in my career. It is a continued step towards the legacy I aspire to build – a legacy that, I hope, will endure beyond my lifetime. This book is a testament to that aspiration and was created with a lot of love.

I hope that you all enjoy it as much as I enjoyed creating it!

Hayden

First published in Great Britain in 2024
by Ilex, an imprint of
Octopus Publishing Group Ltd
Carmelite House
50 Victoria Embankment
London EC4Y 0DZ
www.octopusbooks.co.uk
www.octopusbooksusa.com

An Hachette UK Company
www.hachette.co.uk

Text and illustrations copyright
© Hayden Williams 2024
Design and layout copyright
© Octopus Publishing Group Ltd 2024

Distributed in the US by
Hachette Book Group
1290 Avenue of the Americas
4th and 5th Floors
New York, NY 10105

Distributed in Canada by Canadian Manda
Group, 664 Annette St, Toronto, Ontario,
Canada M6S 2C8

All rights reserved. No part of this work may be reproduced or utilized in any form or by any means, electronic or mechanical, including photocopying, recording or by any information storage and retrieval system, without the prior written permission of the publisher.

Hayden Williams asserts the moral right to be identified as the author of this work.

ISBN 978-1-78157-958-9

A CIP catalogue record for this book is available from the British Library.

Printed and bound in China

10 9 8 7 6 5 4 3 2 1

Publisher: Alison Starling
Consultant Editorial Director: Ellie Corbett
Managing Editor: Rachel Silverlight
Editorial Assistant: Ellen Sleath
Art Director: Ben Gardiner
Production Manager: Caroline Alberti